this
world
from
my
2 eyez

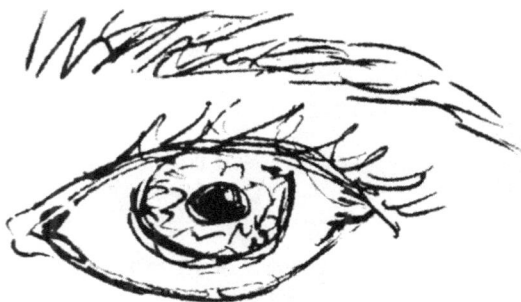

a collection of poems by

REESE LIEBERMAN

For my family

Contents

Be Unafraid

His Own Reflection

Questions of the Universe

The Tree Does Not Worry, Neither Should You

Recipe 2 Success

Foreword

About four years ago I received a phone call from my quiet, sensitive, eleven-year-old granddaughter, Reese. She shared three poems she had written. I was surprised by their depth. Little did I know then, that this was only the beginning of greater things to come. Every week or two for the past four years I have received new poems. We would discuss the ideas and the beauty of each of her creations. Each week I became more amazed at the sophistication and energy in her writings.

Her constant passion with her study and writing of poetry was never ending. She went to sleep with pen and paper by her side. The ocean, the stars, a sunset, a song all were among the triggers for an explosion of ideas and emotion.

This is now my opportunity to thank Reese
for allowing me to participate in her exquisite
journey. I look forward to the rest to be unveiled
over time. This book, I'm sure, is just the start
of much more to come.

Ron Lieberman (my grandfather)

Introduction

Poetry is not a dead language, or something only meant to be understood by those with a college degree. Complexity is not what makes poetry the beautiful thing that it is. Poetry is meant to be read by everybody. Poetry has been a part of society for as far back as historians can dig. It has evolved countless times, from epic poems to haikus, to the sonnets of Shakespeare's time, to spoken word, poetry presents itself in many forms. It can even be found in a get-well card or the lyrics of a song. But no matter what form it takes, the purpose of poetry will never change. Poetry is the notation by a single poet of a feeling or experience shared by many.

this book is meant for people of all ages. if you can relate to it, this is for you. if you can enjoy it, this is for you. if this book makes you feel something, this is for you. i hope as you read, this book brings a smile to your face and perhaps even a little laughter. i hope when you read this book it makes you think. i hope it helps you to see the beauty in things. and most of all, i hope it inspires you to do anything and everything you want to do. (chase your dreams. be happy. life is too short not to.)

This World From My 2 Eyez

I like to think that this world is just 1 big puzzle,
that needs every single 1 of us to be complete
but it's constantly changing and rearranging
like cars on a busy street
Some parts are growing old, others are growing new
like treadmarks and dark patches of concrete
and every time we change it changes with us,
me and you
and the countless other me's and you's
The change of a tiny speck of green to a tiny
speck of blue
may not sound like much,
but if you look to the bigger
you will see even a small change changes the
whole picture

A note from the author:

*As you read you will see that I have
written notes alongside many of my poems,
this is because I want you, the reader,
to know what I was thinking or feeling
at the time when I was writing these poems.
This book is meant for those who know me best
and those whom I've never met.*

BE UNAFRAID

Take The Plunge

With all the things that could possibly scare you
considered -
I believe you should take the plunge -
no, I dare you to take the jump

of all the things that could possibly get
in your way
why should you be one?

---

*I wrote this poem when I was feeling afraid, I re-read it
whenever I am feeling this way.*

Dear Future,

I am not afraid of you
We've met before
and I made it through

Fear of Being Judged

There's this funny little thing called the fear
of being judged
when you try to sleep at night it
keeps you up
it whispers in your ear that you
are not enough
like any other fear, it is a waste of our precious
time under the sun
like any other fear, it is faced by everyone
like any other fear, it takes courage
to overcome

2 B Unafraid

I could run from my fears
and never come back
I could be gone just like that
but that is not being fearless
that is not being brave
we must face what scares us
in order 2 B unafraid

Fearless

It is possible to be fearless
for when you are being brave
you are too busy experiencing the present
to be afraid

Like Midnight

Midnight is unafraid
of silence and of shade
in fact the darkness
is where he's always played
He never waits
for the scary things to fade
He has tripped and fallen
and even lost his way
yet he never hid
from the place where he laid
In spite of the reasons to run,
always he stayed
like midnight I am unafraid

The Echoes

Our actions speak volumes
that transcend hours and rooms
They don't simply drift away —
moments pass but our actions remain

So if you had the power to speak
with the voice of eternity
what would you say?

"What we do in life echoes in eternity"
— *Maximus,* Gladiator *(2000)*

Reese Lieberman

Anchored In Me

The darkness doesn't look so dark
when you look up at the night sky
and see the stars

The waves don't look so tall
when you lift your head up before
they crash and fall

This world isn't so big, this world
isn't so small
when you are just you - you are not
afraid at all

---

*When I wrote this poem I felt completely and utterly
unafraid, and I wanted to capture that feeling. Now when
I re-read it that is exactly how I feel, not afraid at all.*

His Own
Reflection

The Sun

He watched the rain pour
he felt the wind blow
He stepped in a puddle on the ground
and wondered if he had a place
in this world
Was he the sunshine breaking up
the clouds
or in that puddle was he bound
to drown?

The weight of the world sat heavy
on his shoulders
Could he break through it
and if he did would the clouds
turn out to weigh a million pounds?

Reese Lieberman

He felt like a plastic bag,
displaced by the wind
soaked by the rain
Could he end this cycle
of powerlessness and pain?
He had always longed for somebody
to help him, to pull him out of this mess
In this pouring rain he had always longed
  for the sun
then the skies cleared, the storm
was done
he felt a warmth he hadn't felt in months
the person he had always needed
is who he had become
  all along he was the one

There is no spoon.

Light in Dark Places

He looks into the water
and thinks "could this be it?"
the darkness he once feared
and now he's facing it
He looks into the distance
just above the horizon of tar
he sees a single
shining star
and he knows that there is light
in even the darkest of places
just as there is hope
in even the saddest of faces
He will do anything but
give up
A tree can be burned alive
and with every ounce of strength it has left
it will rise

Nature's cycle repeats
again and again
truthfully there is no end
Likewise
he opens his eyes
every golden morning
and each dark dawn
and when the sun comes
more often than not his fears are gone

Not Without Darkness

He is resilient
and broken all at once
He looks to the future
without forgetting who he was
He knows not light
without darkness
He looks to the sky
and below he sees a mess
He is brave
and he is so scared
that he will not make it out ok
He is porcelain
but not without cracks
He holds his head high
in spite of everything he lacks
Dark nights
don't scare him anymore
cuz he's never lived
a life without darkness before

Life in Color

He goes places others are too scared to go
he looks to the ugly parts of this world most are
afraid of
some people rarely stray from the things that
they know
people who have only known hatred rarely love
likewise those who have been cared for are most
likely to
care for others
You'd never know there was a world outside
your bedroom
if you always hid beneath the covers
Some live life in black and white
he lives his in many colors
He's not afraid and he's not ashamed
of what most people do not dare look at
for he has known cruelty his whole life,
he's also known care

he's not afraid to look back
he knows that both beauty and ugly are
everywhere
and he's not afraid to stare

Inspired by The House of the Scorpion *by Nancy Farmer.*

In Time

He stands at the edge
and contemplates what comes next
He is brave but
life is tough
Sometimes he fears that he is not enough
He stares at the edge
and decides to rise above
the only question is how;
how will he reach his potential now?
No doubt he will rise above
but how will he get through this life that's
tough?
Is he at the bottom of the barrel
too hard to climb up
or a low point on the coaster
going steadily in time up?

In time he will realize that he is enough
and though life is tough
he will rise above.

Wanderings of the Mind

Time is harsh
must life be?
He looks deep from the waters, drowning in
themselves, to the marsh
Hating is not done with a stone-cold but a heavy
heart
with the urgency and the whispers of fear that
tear one apart
and rebuild them with resentment
for them, time is no longer in the present
He looks to his own reflection in the water,
the clearest image he'll ever see of himself is in
the hugging waves and their slaughter
Slowly, he looks to the skies
and he realizes it has always been there to
realize
He feels a rushing in his veins as he looks upon
the waters;

he sees a five tipped star. . . floating
He looks to the edge of the river and he sees
rocks clinging to the roughness,
paying for that choice in the price of eroding
He shuts his eyes with a shiver; we human rocks
are the ones who poison ourselves
with loathing and foreboding
and us human leaves or stars go through this life
floating, without even knowing
The whispers of the wind ask him:
"Are you a leaf or are you a rock?"
He reaches into his pocket and pulls out his
harsh clock,
he opens his eyes, but he does not see the
horrible hands, nor the floaters nor the settlers
He sees himself and he knows that he is better
He sees the colors and the movement, he sees
both potential and room for improvement
Again, he opens his eyes
this time not to his world but the outside one
his decision is unsaid but nonetheless done

Reese Lieberman

He puts his watch back in his pocket,
he looks above, to the sunshine rocket
Again, he witnesses the lost ones and the
settlers, this time without a shiver
He whispers to the wind "I am a river."

DREAMS

Leaving Neverland

Spinning endlessly in no particular direction
I am suspended in the air
with a blurry perception
and a creeping fear that I may not
ever land
I'll just float, like dust
is this what life is supposed to be like
in Neverland?
Do our dreams shape our reality
or do we let reality shape our dreams?
Have we simply forgotten who we once
longed to be?
Do we have this world in the palm of our
hand
or have we grown comfortable filling our
palms with sand?

Inspired by Peter Pan *by J.M. Barrie.*

When I Am No Longer 14

When I'm no longer fourteen
will this year feel like nothing more than a fever
dream?
From which I long ago awoken
Will these words be nothing more than a token
or will I stay true to past words I have spoken?
When I'm no longer naive
will I still find things in which to believe?
Will I find ways to give more than I receive?
Will I forget what it's like to be a child
or will I be wise but nonetheless wild?
When I've seen many things
will I still imagine that I could grow wings
and fly away to where the bluebird sings?
Will I still have calluses from my guitar strings?
Will I forget the things that truly matter
or will I stay true even if someday my heart
becomes shattered?

Will I still dream
when I'm no longer fourteen?

Written at age 14.

Midnight Sunrise

The thing about humans is;
we see what we want to see
we are creatures that live somewhere
between dreams & reality
If we want to see blue skies
what do you think we'll see?
& how about a midnight sunrise,
cuz there's magic that lives
behind our eyes
If we want to fly
we'll look below us & see a sky
But the thing is;
if you don't have a vision
the magic will never work
There's something about people who dream
that makes reality go berserk
If a dreamer wants to fly
suddenly below them, they will find a sky

but some people never seem to shut or open
their eyes
& they miss out on the magic of the midnight
sunrise

Inner Light

Find the thing that brings you light
and once you find it chase endlessly after it
and when the skies come to tell you
that it is night
and you need a little brightness
reach over to the side of your bed and
flick on the light switch

Writing is the thing that brings me light. On nights when I can't sleep I reach over to the table beside my bed and grab paper and a pen, and scribble words that may or may not make any sense. Actually flicking on the light switch works as well.

Chase Your Dreams

You planted seeds
where no flowers
have ever grown before,
then you forgot
to water them
and they grew no more —

you must chase
your dreams
like a blackhole chases
a galaxy
in order to make them a
reality

Who U Should B

Don't let the world tell U
who U should B
Nobody knows better than U
the things that U dream
& when faced with the eyes
of misery
nobody knows if U would run,
scream,
or look evil in the eyes like
U could conquer it in Ur sleep
So don't let the world tell U
who U should B
Maybe U can fly
maybe U have the power of invisibility
but 1 thing is certain
if U don't try U will never know
what could B
if U don't try
U will never succeed

Falling Stars

There is a calling coming from the distance
        can you hear it?
The stars have not disappeared yet
The sea continues to wash over the shore
There it is, can you hear the calling
once more?
As the stars dance across the night sky
and the sea rises as though trying to fly
can you feel it?
The calling that comes from the distance
like a wound that bleeds begging you
        to heal it
Don't be afraid, for the stars continue to shine
bright
The waves crash in the sea as the cosmos
shed their light
like a bird shedding its feathers
they drift, at last untethered

Reese Lieberman

There's a calling like the whistle of a distant
wind
do you feel it against your skin?
Do not fear it,
        let it in
The stars have not disappeared yet
they shine in the night sky
as though to protect us from the darkness
where dreams are born and dreams die
that's it — that's the calling
watch out — the stars are falling
even the sun —
reach out and catch one

---

*Written while listening to "Tonglen" by
Georg Deuter.*

Dreamer's Sky

You can reach the sky
You can go as high
As you'd like
Where the lightning strikes
Up in the clouds
Away from the crowds
You can reach stars and galaxies
No matter how high
You can fly
The question is, what is your sky?

A Dream (15)

Fifteen and on the brink of a dream
I don't want to awaken until it becomes
clear to me
so please let me sleep

Fifteen and captivated by the things
that I have seen
I don't want to awaken until I become
what I am meant to be
so please let me sleep

Fifteen
and only beginning to dream
like a ship chases after the sea
and a villain plots up a scheme
so do not wake me,
for I am not asleep
and this isn't a dream

---

*Written at age 15. This was meant to answer the questions
asked in "When I Am No Longer 14."*

INFINITE
POSSIBILITIES

Infinite Possibilities

Impossible does not make sense to me
I am matter and energy
held together by the forces of gravity
Some might call it a miracle —
I call it extraordinary
Life is the product of one in a billion
possibilities
with low probability
and yet when you step outside —
fish swim in the sea
up above in the sky birds glide
within your chest, a heart beats
that's why impossible does not make sense
to me
The number of possibilities
is the only thing which we know for certain
reaches infinity

Child of Stardust

I am a child of stardust and the soil
beneath my feet
I am a willow with a heartbeat
A wildfire with intensity and heat
A miracle below both skies and ceilings
with dreams, fears, and feelings
I am where stardust meets planet
earth, I am a human being

Leaf in the Sky

I am a leaf in the sky
fallen from a tree, I am not meant to fly
but here I am in the wind up high
in the tunnels of the cosmos
I am a seed where nothing grows
This is not where I am meant to be
but here I am, held only by the fragile
fingers of fate
an exile of love is also an exile of hate
So here I am and here I wait
for I am a leaf in the sky
fallen from a tree, and yet I fly
as though I was born to defy

Feather in the Wind

Like a feather gliding through the wind
it serves its purpose
but not in the way most people would expect
all it is meant to do is fly
just look at it gliding through the sky
Some might look at it and say it's a
lost cause
others won't even bat an eye
and some might marvel at the way
it defies gravity's laws
Some people are like feathers gliding
through the wind
and though they don't end exactly where
they begin
they surely are brave, free
and serving their purpose, wouldn't you agree?

Things are not always as they seem.

Bird With Broken Wings

They thought it was just missing a feather,
so they sent it off into the blue
The little bird, with the funny walk
everybody thought they knew
Turns out it had a broken wing —
and guess what?
It flew.

Set in Stone

Even what's set in stone
isn't really set in stone
concrete can be molded,
to build a home
build a throne
for your backbone
Full can be the stomachs
once starved
and even what's set in stone
can be carved

Nothing is impossible.

Impossible Things

Trying to do impossible things
is like trying to grow while being a leaf inside
the wind
feeling cold even when sunlight's touch
is upon your skin
wishing you could win,
but failing again and again
being submerged in water only to find you don't
know how to swim
taking countless flights only to end up where
you've been
defying gravity in the wind
only to find you don't have wings
and falling again
that's what it's like trying to do impossible
things
but they are only impossible until you realize
impossible is not what cannot be done
but what hasn't been

Against the Odds

Leave the past to whomever lives there
Beneath our stomachs, skin, and hair
all we are is breathing air
You can look further if you dare
past our beating hearts
an ending comes, a beginning starts
We are matter and energy
come together to form life you see
We are particles and waves you and me
with air between
The ethereal about which you dream
comes to life right before your very eyes
within your hands, within your thighs
The odds are thin and sharp as a knife
we are matter and energy come together to
form life

If Artists Could Paint The Sky

If artists could paint the sky
If a sculptor could shape the human heart and
eye
maybe we wouldn't take for granted
the world shared by you and I
If musicians could compose the wind
and poets could show us where to begin
maybe we would better appreciate
the world we live within
and if artists could paint the sky
what could possibly be impossible for
you and I?

THE HUMAN
EXPERIENCE

The Human Condition

The human condition
isn't a mindset it's a mission
we're always wishin
and fishin
trying 2 catch some better days
trying 2 get 2 a better place
The human condition
is having a vision
Searching 4 light
so much so we get lost in the night
until we find stars that shine bright
cuz then we're fine, right?
Right or wrong the power of the nature
of the human mind is strong
The human condition
is trying 2 belong
the problem is we often fail 2 listen
2 busy singing our own song

and getting dizzy when the night is long
The human condition
is wishin
4 the dawn
then realizin the daylight doesn't
make a difference
we must learn 2 carry on
and yet we continue 2 look 2 the
horizon in the distance
like light has some gravitational pull
on our existence
like we R children of the sun
The human condition
is finding hope where there is none
and sometimes a mother lifts a car
off of her son

Moving Forward

The most important move we can make as
living, breathing
beings is forward
Break the boxes
Stop living in other people's idea
Live the life you want to live
Nobody else will ever get the chance to be ya
so take what is yours
& after you have learned to take learn to give
Break the boxes you live within
because it is you that must decide the kind of
world
you want to live in
& it is your responsibility to make that a reality
When you are in a sea
there is only one thing that matters
& that is moving forward
Though sometimes life feels like vertigo

Though sometimes you may be moving slow
Sometimes life may feel like wading through
deep waters
in the dead of night
the sun will rise & you will find your way in
daylight
shoreward
Living, breathing beings must keep moving
forward

Mentally I
n
c
l
i
n
e
d

What if most of the time
what people say is right
isn't really right
I may be lost inside my mind
I am mentally inclined
but I swear people will always
try to put us in boxes
　　　I swear it's not fair
for our souls are made of stardust
not rectangular nor square

and what if when we dive deeper
into what we feel
and further from what people call the truth
we are actually closer to
      what is real

The human experience
is waves not straight lines
people will try to put us in boxes
but there are places in our minds
that go deeper than our skulls
for we have not rectangular
nor triangular souls
we are stardust, we are circles
that never end
people that deny this are people
that pretend

There is always more to people than meets the eye.
Nobody is simply smart, or funny, or loud, or shy. We are
all too complex to be that easily defined.

Poets Always Talk About the Stars

Poets always talk about looking up at the stars
and then once you finally do, don't they make
you feel ever so terribly small?
Like the ground beneath your feet could be torn
apart
and the cosmos wouldn't fall
Like your beating heart
is only a whisper in the background of the noise
of the rest of the world which you are only a
small part of
Like to be human is to be an observer of the
great beauty that lies above
We are small, yet we are everything to each
other
maybe looking up at the stars teaches us to love
one another

I am one of those poets who always talks about the stars.

Beauty Exists

Beauty lies in the depths
  of what is unnatural
   unpure
and most don't consider beautiful
Beauty lies in the depths
of places where it is
   most hard to find
Beauty lies in the heart,
    soul and mind
Beauty lies in the depths
of places so dark and
    ugly you must
be looking for it or
   you will never see it
and lastly beauty cannot
  be tarnished by
anything except for
the notion that
    you don't believe it
    exists

Love Is Not Logic

The thing about humans is
we can have no logical reason to hope
and yet we do
for hope is not about what is
it's about finding a way to make
it through

And so through the darkest nights
we wait for the skies to turn blue
Through the deepest lies
we wait to hear the truth
because logic is not enough
for those who believe in love

Puzzle Pieces

This universe is a puzzle
and I am just a single piece
There simply are no boundaries
unless you decide to build walls
but you will find when one of them falls
that space is an endless place
there are absolutely no limits to
how many stars can shine
and we've got pieces of them in
our minds
though they may be scattered like coins
in a street
Purpose cannot be stolen and it is
not a game in which to compete
remember a puzzle needs every single
piece to be complete

Superman

Dedicated to my grandmother, who is one of the most empathetic and caring souls I will ever have the privilege to know.

Did superman
ever need a helping hand?
What if he were 2 fly away
and never land?
Fly away without a plan
If U were superman
would U gaze upon this world
like it was UR number 1 fan
or would U escape in a
getaway van
and go as far away as U
possibly can
or would U try 2 explain things
so people would understand
that super's just a title

and U R just a man
2 some U R an idol
but this isn't really what U had planned
and U couldn't fulfill the people's
every demand
or would U just accept the statue
that someone built 4 U
and shake the mayor's hand
while reality ate away at U
cuz U were trying as hard as U can
but life isn't easy, even when
it is grand
Does superman
ever need a helping hand?
If U were superman
would U fly away and never land?

Little Things

All those little things that used to scare me
are no longer scary
All those little things that I use to ignore,
like the sunsets on the shore
and the stars above you and me —
are all I see
My old fears are so out of reach
All those little things that used to matter don't
I could ask what if — but I won't
I won't spoil my todays with the troubles
of my tomorrows
nor will I pretend I've got no sorrows
but I've learned by now
it is the little things that matter
like going outside when the rain is pouring
down
and looking up to the clouds
while lying on the ground —

it's not about what you are doing, it's about
how you do it
that's why when a door is open I'll be running
through it
I will watch the world from behind my window
then I'll step outside to feel the wind blow
for it does not matter what you are doing,
but how you do it
you can exist or you can experience things —
the good, the bad, the beautiful, and that
which ends in ruin
for that's what it means to be human

---

*We live not for the momentous occasions but for the little
things in life.*

Golden

Gold might glow to the ends of the Earth
but superstars shine when the night is
at its darkest
and you've lost all sense of direction
And in the spring daisies bloom
after the long, cold winter, changing
our perception
reminding us of the warm sunlight
and the golden sunsets that put
our minds at ease,
and gently whisk us off to sleep
Gold might glow to the ends of the Earth
and rich are those who sold it
but never-fading are the golden eyes
that behold it

Reese Lieberman

Thick and Thin

Through the thick where we begin
we will learn to swim
And glide through the wind
take our time in the thin
Even though we don't have wings or fins
we have hearts and skin
So we stay afloat in the sea
and soar in the wind
Realizin' it's not about the win
but keeping your head up when you can't swim
Looking up to the stars when the night is dim
and finding the light within
Survivin' through thick and thin

Human Below These Ceilings

I don't know what tomorrow brings
I do know that if someday I grow wings
I won't live below these ceilings
that presently block my view of the sky —
if I grow wings I shall fly
If I become the sea I shall rise
but I am human, and I don't want to
cause ships to capsize
and if I wake up as a bird tomorrow
surely I will reach the skies
but I am human, I cannot fly
I haven't got wings
I am not too large to live below these ceilings

I think some people are always wanting to escape, to leave. Always searching for a change of scenery, as though their happiness is defined by a place rather than themselves, but this is not the case.

Coastline (Harmony Lives)

In the midst of dark waters
beneath raging storms
     that will not be silenced
harmony lives
     on the edge
of serenity and violence
In the midst of dark waters
beneath raging storms
     is a single beam of light
on the edge
     of recklessness and calm
where harmony lives her life
In the midst of dark waters
beneath raging storms
and beaches that have been
the destination
of many of man's battles over time
     on the edge
of peace and chaos
harmony is the coastline

A New Beginning

Rising up from stormy seas
I let the wind take hold of me
into what lies above
Just like the tree
letting go of its leaves
Rising up into the autumn breeze
The earth lets go of me
My eyes are up as I ascend from
the ship sinking sea
I look to the clouds as sunset's
color slowly bleeds
Rising up into the place where
I'll be free
I stare into the setting sun
My time's not up —
it's only just begun

QUESTIONS OF
THE UNIVERSE

Questions of the Universe

Dedicated to my grandfather, who has
endlessly inspired me to keep asking questions,
and to always keep learning, as well as writing.

Questions sit in the wake of humble darkness
like a solar system without stars
Questions wait patiently like tire-less cars
for the repairman to come along
because questions are broken pieces of the
universe
that wait to be put where they belong

Questions sit in humble darkness
like a crescent moon without stars
they wait patiently like driverless cars
for a valet to come along
because questions are broken pieces of the
universe
that wait to be put where they belong

Questions sit in the wake of humble darkness
like a ribcage without a heart
Some men ask questions in the hopes to repair
this broken universe
others intend to tear it apart

If Darkness Was a Sun

What if darkness was a Sun?
Would any work get done?
Would frogs and minnows have any fun?
Would honey bees be black?
Would time turn back?
Would the equator turn frosty?
Would indoor heaters be costly?
Would snails crawl back into their shells?
Would London no longer ring its bells?
Would books stay locked up on their shelves?
Would butterflies keep to themselves?
Would highways stand still?
Would a bird fly into a windowsill?
Would day be night and night be day
or would that nonsense just go away?
Would anybody ever move on
or would they be too afraid to step out
on their own front lawn?

Would they even run?
And would the moon be indifferent
if darkness was a Sun?

Step Outside

Are the stars meant to guide us
or to hide us
from the great expanse that resides
above our heads?
Why is it that we can't face it
when we are asleep inside our beds?
Why do we search for light
when really we need rest?
Why do we need beaming stars when
each of us has a heart beating
in our chest?
When will we realize that the only light
we need is inside?
When will we step out of the place
where we hide?

What Is Precious

What is pure
compared to the soul
that has been withered,
stepped on like blades of grass
and regrown?
What is gold
compared to the phoenix
that has crashed, fallen, burned
and been reborn?
What is a diamond
compared to a river
that flows forever
while shaping the world
around it
rather than letting the world
shape it?
What is a crystal
compared to a pond

or an open sea
that turns raindrops
into rising tides
where the greatest of
storms form?
What is precious
in a world where greatness
is born?

Reese Lieberman

Have You Ever Heard?

Have you ever heard of a bird
that decided not to sing
left its nest
and clipped its own wings?

Have you ever told a river
which way to flow?
Have you told the snow
which way to go?
Did you once tell the skies to be blue
and did they ever listen to you?

Have you ever heard of a rose
that decided not to grow?

This poem was inspired by The Rose That Grew From Concrete *by Tupac Shakur (aka 2Pac).*

Universe in Us

The history of the universe
courses through our veins
and breathes through our lungs
The search, called space exploration
is like a child's curiosity
about where their parents come from
and when we look through those telescopes
searching for answers
not yet found in books on library shelves
we are really just searching for answers
to questions about ourselves

Open Door

We all start out as nothing
the question is, are we capable of evolving into
something more?
Is it possible to find something worth
fighting for?
These are questions I ask, but none of us
can ignore
We are not birds, there isn't one single
answer like learning to soar
but maybe that is the great thing about
being human, being able to explore
to go places no other has ever been before
Sometimes I wonder why man invented
the door
Was it to deepen the divide
which we all feel from time to time?
Or to create a place to hide?
Or maybe the man who invented the door

felt he had adventured to all the places
there are to explore
so he created another, with ceiling and floor
I wonder if he thought this world a mighty bore
or maybe he was filled with curiosity
and wanted to expand it furthermore,
maybe that was his way of learning to soar
after all we all have our own, some are
different than any other ever before
We all start out as nothing
the question is how we choose to turn ourselves
into something more
We all choose what is worth fighting for
and whether we open or shut the door
at each of our souls' very core

On Some Other Night

If the stars don't shine tonight
I'm sure they'll shine some other night
When the headlights are bright
and the highway lanes are tight
If the stars don't shine tonight
I'm sure they'll fall in line some other night when
the moon is at its height and
the sea is quite a sight then
on some other night
I'm sure the stars will shine bright
I'm certain they'll fall in line on another midnight
the headlights may be bright
and the traffic may be tight then
but no doubt the stars will shine another night
will you still be searching
for their light?

It's easy to miss something that isn't there, but it's even easier to miss things that are there.

What is Beautiful?

What does beautiful mean?
Does it mean the setting sun
on the horizon
or daisies in a garden
or the person that you think is pretty
or the evening sky over the sea?
Is beautiful a smile
or a mountain view that lasts for miles?
Is beautiful the things you dream
or is it the things you see
or maybe it's the things you need?
Is beautiful a different thing
every morning you wake up
like the simple act of putting on
a necklace or a ring
or does it mean everything?
Is beautiful the things you dream
or do you have nightmares?

Is beauty the things that spare you
from all the things that scare you?
Is beauty an idea or is it an ideal?
Is beauty dreamed up by architects
or is it the way we feel?

THE TREE
DOES NOT WORRY,
NEITHER SHOULD YOU

The Tree Does Not Worry

The tree does not worry
how it looks without its leaves
nor how they blow in the summer breeze
The tree does not worry
about these things
The tree simply does the things
which it needs
and that is the difference between
the tree and the seeds

The Sunset

The sunset did not scream nor beg for attention
the sunset was simply its ever-changing self
and that's enough to make the world stare
with wonder, excitement, and awe
to write songs of summertime, paint
masterpieces
that look like liquid sunshine on a canvas,
write poetry that touches the soul and frees
the human mind
for the sunset is not without flaw,
perfection is a thing of fantasy but it defies
all law
like it knows its destiny
that's why I long to be like the sunset
simple, yet complex and ever so free

I wrote this after watching a beautiful and inspiring sunset.

Autumn Breath

The wind takes the worries out of my head
until I am nothing more than an
Autumn leaf blowing through the air instead
I am no longer lost in my mind
but drifting in the wind
and when I land I shall not land in an ocean
but a puddle or a swimming pool
alive with tadpoles
It's like I'm a star and I've just escaped
a black hole
or maybe I am Aurora just taking a stroll
for the wind takes the worries out of my head
and I begin to forget all the time
they once stole
I've seldom forgotten my role
The wind takes the worries out of my head
and strips me down to my soul

Rivers Rise

The rivers always rise
There are always changes in the skies
It is harder to identify truth than it is lies
There is only the constant blinking
of wakeful eyes
and knowledge that the sun will rise
That the creature that has lows
also has highs
the one that smiles also cries
the one that lives eventually dies
and that still the rivers rise
Still there is a painter behind the skies
We live in a moment while for the rest
of the world a decade flies
We live in moments yet all creation
is in our eyes
Where there are lows there are highs

Where one lives another dies
and most of all the falling of the skies
are why the rivers relentlessly rise

Nobody Sees It

Light does not exist if no one sees it
Myth is only myth if nobody believes it
Music is nothing but vibrations if no one cares
to listen
Light will not come to you, you must make it
a part of your vision
A helping hand could be reaching out to you,
but it makes
no difference if you don't reach out your own
If you don't smile when you're alone
then company is just a way to pass the time
I'm making this up but there is truth to
my rhyme
Because the light does not exist if nobody sees it
but the caged bird still sings when nobody
frees it

To Have A Beating Heart

Some people only see the darkness,
others only stars
Some people search for headlights,
others look for cars
Some people look too closely at things,
others too far
Why isn't there an in-between?
Why can't we just be where we are?
Why are people always looking
for a missing part?
Why isn't it enough to be living, to be
breathing, to have a beating heart?

Darkness and Light

In the darkest of times
the sun rises
the stars shine
and someone realizes
we need not run
away from the night
there will always be
darkness
and there will always
be light
what we need most
is to find a balance of
them both

Beauty is Born

Beauty is born
and the seeds and sproutlings may be beautiful
but true greatness lies in the tree
that has survived the storm

Beauty is nice to look at
but it is strength that lives when
darkness comes to attack

Beauty awakens in the dawn
but it is courage that keeps on

Beauty is born
but it takes strength and courage
to survive the storm

Stars Don't Shine 4 U & Me

The stars shine on this gloomy night
but R U 2 blind 2 C?
They don't shine 4 U & me
They shine so they can B free
They shine 4 the same reason that
leaves grow from a tree
They shine as waves rise in the sea
but U R 2 blind 2 C
the stars don't shine 4 U & me

They shine because it is their destiny

RECIPE 2 SUCCESS

Recipe 2 Success

There is no victory
if you don't consider yourself
victorious
Often your greatest milestones go
unrecognized
but the dictionary says

<u>Success:</u>
noun 1. the accomplishment of one's
goals

That is the definition
but its meaning?
That is completely up to you
What do you want to do?

Victory is overcoming something,
such as a battle
but success is reaching a goal
success is taking control
success is becoming whole
success is the sidekick of the soul

So, you want to be successful?
First you've got to have a goal

Success is a Ladder

Failure comes in knowing that you could have
done better but didn't
Trying your hardest is success
There are many different levels of success
it is like a ladder
so keep climbing up
and when you think you've climbed high
enough
and you are ready to leave
remember there is still more greatness that
you can achieve

Enter the Void

It does not matter if the door is open,
it does not matter if a hundred doors are open
you are the one who must walk through them

just like how every morning you get the chance
to wake up and seize the day
but it is you who must choose this

the paths have been laid, and for those that
aren't there is brick and cement which can be
forged
the universe is there, enter the void
and decide whether you will be a spark, a torch,
or if you will light up a whole entire forest
Are you merely a backup singer or will you
sing the chorus?

we all wake up every single day
inside of different bones inside a different home
yet the same question is asked for all of us:
do you want to let the day pass you by
or do you want to own it?

if your answer is the latter you must apply
that choice to every single moment

"There is no such thing as tough. There is trained and untrained. Now which are you?"
Man on Fire *(2004)*

Roots + Wings

It is possible to have both
roots and wings:
Wings will help you to fly
into the unknown
Roots will guide you
on your way back home

Success

Strength exists in becoming strong
The ending is not where the success is,
the action of becoming is where
            triumph belongs

Reese Lieberman

In Style

Dedicated to Kobe Bryant

I might be an exile
I'll still go out in style
drop the mic to the tiles
I won't be going for a while
I've still got many miles
to go, but when I go
I'ma go out in style

An exit
is an echo of the way
you exist
I will go with a tightened fist
My shots will not be missed

I might be on fire
Situations dire
I won't be a cryer
Reality is an empire
and I sit atop its throne
This world is mine to roam

I might be on fire
Situations dire
but I'ma climb higher
I've still got a while
but when I go my last mile
I might be an exile
I might be on trial
Still I'ma drop the mic to the tile
cuz Kobe taught me to go out in style

Acknowledgements

I am eternally grateful for everybody who has been
there for me, helped me,
read my poems countless times,
believed in me ever since I started writing,
and motivated me to be the best that I can be,
thank you,
you are my biggest inspirations

A special thank you to my sisters, Kyra and Taylor,
this book is 100x better than it would have been
without your help.

P.S. Once my grandfather made me promise to never
stop writing. I won't.

About the Author

REESE LIEBERMAN is a teen poet. She has
been writing poetry since she was eleven years
old. This is her first published poetry collection
of many more to come.

For more of her writing, visit @reesewith3e.s
on Instagram, YouTube, or TikTok.